COMMON BONDS

What do the numbers 3, 7, 8, 40, 50, and 60 have in common that no other number has?

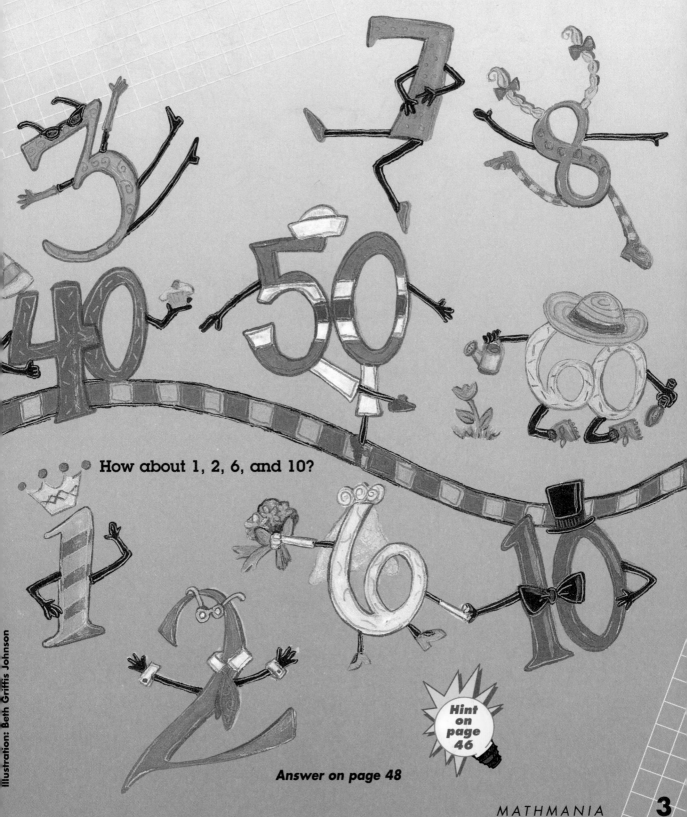

How about 1, 2, 6, and 10?

Hint on page 46

Answer on page 48

Illustration: Beth Griffis Johnson

COUNTING SHEEP

quietly counting the number of sheep here.

Illustration: David Helton

Hint on page 46

MATHMANIA

5

SIMONE SAYS

Simone built two too many squares for the shelves to display her rock collection. Rearrange three different sticks to make only five squares, with no leftover sticks.

Illustration: R. Michael Palan

Answer on page 48

TAKE OFF

One plane doesn't belong in each row. Can you take off the wrong number and replace it with a correct number?

A. 5, 2, 8, 11, 13, 17, 20

B. 40, 45, 50, 55, 56, 65

C. 31, 27, 25, 19, 15, 11

D. 3, 1½, 4½, 5, 7½, 10½, 9

Illustration: Jim Downer

Answer on page 48

EYE TEST

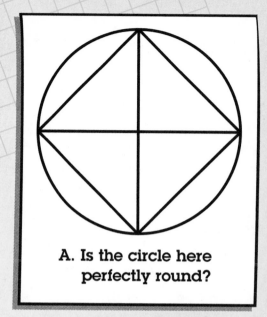

A. Is the circle here perfectly round?

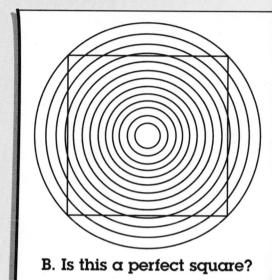

B. Is this a perfect square?

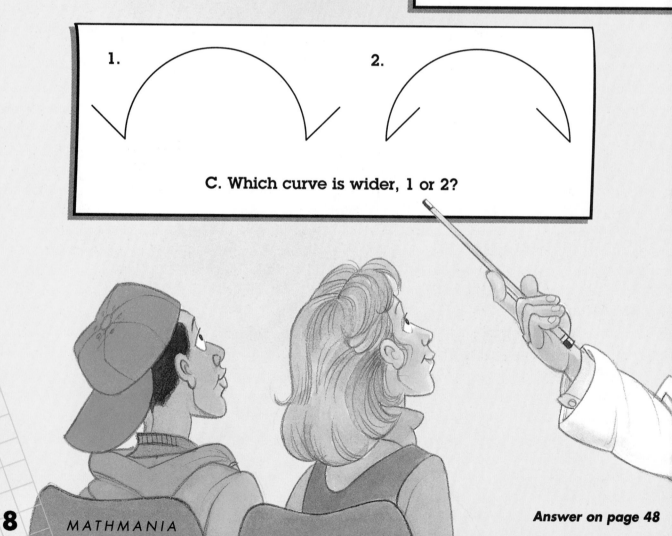

1.

2.

C. Which curve is wider, 1 or 2?

Answer on page 48

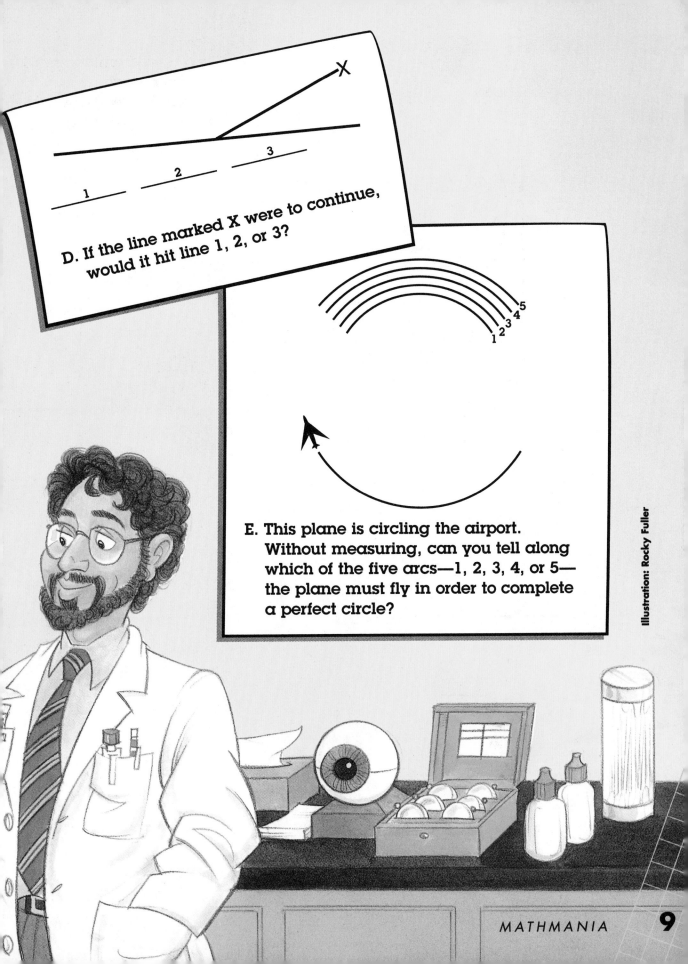

D. If the line marked X were to continue, would it hit line 1, 2, or 3?

E. This plane is circling the airport. Without measuring, can you tell along which of the five arcs—1, 2, 3, 4, or 5— the plane must fly in order to complete a perfect circle?

Illustration: Rocky Fuller

IN GOOD SHAPE

Hint on page 46

Can you tell which number belongs in each shape? The same number will always go inside its matching shape.

A. △ + ◯ = 12   △ − ◯ = 6

B. ☆ + ⬠ = 17   ☆ − ⬠ = 3

C. ▢ + ⬭ = 14   ▢ − ⬭ = 2

D. ⬡ + ◇ = 20   ⬡ − ◇ = 12

E. ▢ + ▱ = 13   ▢ − ▱ = 3

F. ⏢ + ⬠ = 18   ⏢ − ⬠ = 4

Answer on page 48

DOTS A LOT

Connect these numbers in order from the lowest number to the highest to see who's hanging around.

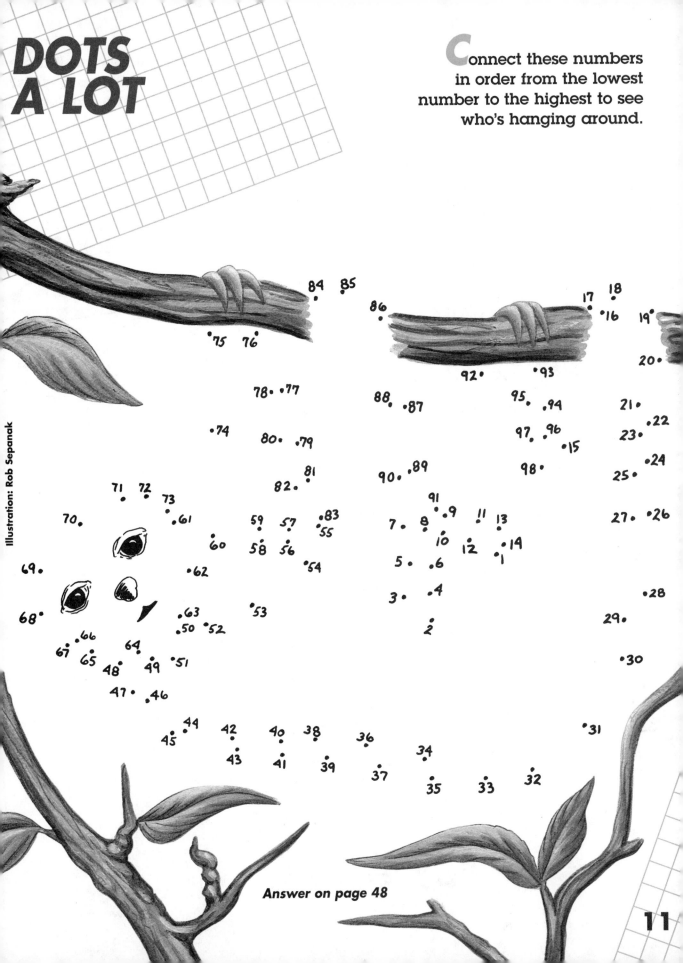

Illustration: Rob Sepanak

Answer on page 48

each car and match it to an answer number to find the right space.

CRUNCH AND MUNCH

Hint on page 46

Betty, Bobby, Billie, and Bud usually eat a total of 8 ounces of cereal for breakfast each morning. Can you tell how many breakfasts they can get from each box of cereal on the table?

Purple Peanut Puffs
2 pounds

FLAKY FLAKES
3½ pounds

MILK

Chocolate Sugar Screamers
2½ pounds

Mini Micro Marshmallows
48 ounces

Seaweed and Succotash Smacks
64 ounces

FAMOUS NAME

If you connect the dots in the order listed, you will find the name of the person described in this autobiography.

Illustration: Kit Wray

Many people think that I was the greatest inventor of all time. Even though I had little formal schooling, I patented more than 1,000 inventions in my lifetime. Some of these inventions included the light bulb, the phonograph, the mimeograph machine, the early telephone transmitter, and the motion picture projector. I even filmed the very first version of *Frankenstein* to demonstrate my process.

```
   A B C D E F G H I J K L M N
1  · · · · · · · · · · · · · ·
2  · · · · · · · · · · · · · ·
3  · · · · · · · · · · · · · ·
4  · · · · · · · · · · · · · ·
5  · · · · · · · · · · · · · ·
6  · · · · · · · · · · · · · ·
```

A1-C1 F1-G1 K1-L1 M1-N1 A4-B4 F4-G4 H4-I4 F3-G3 M3-N3
A6-B6 F6-G6 H6-I6 D2-E2 K2-L2 A5-B5 F5-G5 M1-M2 F4-F5
B1-B3 D1-D3 E1-E3 F1-F3 G1-G3 H1-H3 J1-J3 K1-K3 L1-L3
A4-A6 C4-C6 E4-E6 H4-H6 I4-I6 J4-J6 K4-K6 H1-I2 N2-N3
C4-D5 J4-K6 I2-J1 M2-N2 C6-D5 G5-G6

MONEY-MAKER

Shade in the square that contains the value of each of the following coin combinations.

4 dimes and 3 pennies
4 nickels and 6 pennies
2 quarters, 2 dimes, and 4 pennies
3 dimes, 1 nickel, and 2 pennies
1 quarter and 6 nickels
2 quarters and 13 pennies
3 quarters and 2 pennies
7 nickels
1 dime, 2 nickels, and 3 pennies
3 quarters and 2 nickels
1 quarter and 2 pennies
4 nickels and 4 pennies
2 quarters, 3 nickels, and 2 pennies
1 quarter and 4 dimes
2 quarters, 2 dimes, and 3 pennies
5 dimes and 3 pennies
6 dimes and 16 pennies
2 dimes and 1 nickel
9 nickels
1 dime and 1 nickel
3 quarters
3 dimes and 3 pennies

The shaded squares should make sense once you are done.

Hint on page 46

1	2	3	4	5	6	7	8	9	10
11	12	13	14	15	16	17	18	19	20
21	22	23	24	25	26	27	28	29	30
31	32	33	34	35	36	37	38	39	40
41	42	43	44	45	46	47	48	49	50
51	52	53	54	55	56	57	58	59	60
61	62	63	64	65	66	67	68	69	70
71	72	73	74	75	76	77	78	79	80
81	82	83	84	85	86	87	88	89	90
91	92	93	94	95	96	97	98	99	100

Answer on page 49

LET'S RE-COOP

Farmer Jean has four chickens and only three pens as shown here. How can she put the pens together so that each chicken will have its own pen?

Hint on page 46

Answer on page 49

ALL ALIKE

Turn each row of numbers into an equation. You must place two different function signs, either ×, −, ÷, or +, between the numbers. All six rows will have the same two signs, and all six rows will equal the same final amount.

$$3 \underline{\quad} 6 \underline{\quad} 8 = \underline{\quad}$$

$$5 \underline{\quad} 4 \underline{\quad} 10 = \underline{\quad}$$

$$2 \underline{\quad} 9 \underline{\quad} 8 = \underline{\quad}$$

$$7 \underline{\quad} 2 \underline{\quad} 4 = \underline{\quad}$$

$$6 \underline{\quad} 5 \underline{\quad} 20 = \underline{\quad}$$

$$3 \underline{\quad} 5 \underline{\quad} 5 = \underline{\quad}$$

Answer on page 49

Hint on page 46

DIGIT DOES IT

Illustration: Joe Boddy

Answer on page 49

He's on the scene before the curtain goes up, and he has a clue. One musical note was left behind. Can you decipher it and help the Inspector gather the clues?

Hint on page 46

$\overline{1}\ \overline{20}\ \overline{19}\ \overline{18}$, $\overline{17}\ \overline{16}\ \overline{15}\ \overline{14}\ \overline{20}\ \overline{13}\ \overline{12}\ \overline{11}\ \overline{18}$ $\overline{1}\ \overline{17}\ \overline{10}\ \overline{17}\ \overline{12}$

$\overline{9}\ \overline{11}\ \overline{8}\ \overline{7}\ \overline{20}$ $\overline{6}\ \overline{11}\ \overline{18}\ \overline{16}\ \overline{20}\ \overline{1}$ $\overline{17}\ \overline{16}$ $\overline{15}\ \overline{11}$ $\overline{17}$ $\overline{5}\ \overline{8}\ \overline{15}\ \overline{12}$ $\overline{4}\ \overline{3}\ \overline{20}\ \overline{20}$

$\overline{12}\ \overline{11}$ $\overline{2}\ \overline{20}$ $\overline{17}\ \overline{16}\ \overline{15}\ \overline{12}\ \overline{18}\ \overline{8}\ \overline{5}\ \overline{20}\ \overline{16}\ \overline{12}\ \overline{19}\ \overline{3}$ $\overline{17}\ \overline{16}$ $\overline{13}\ \overline{19}\ \overline{12}\ \overline{13}\ \overline{6}\ \overline{17}\ \overline{16}\ \overline{10}$ $\overline{5}\ \overline{20}$

$\overline{3}\ \overline{11}\ \overline{11}\ \overline{21}$ $\overline{15}\ \overline{6}\ \overline{19}\ \overline{18}\ \overline{14}$ $\overline{19}\ \overline{16}\ \overline{1}$ $\overline{12}\ \overline{18}\ \overline{9}$ $\overline{12}\ \overline{11}$ $\overline{15}\ \overline{20}\ \overline{20}$

$\overline{12}\ \overline{6}\ \overline{20}$ $\overline{B}\ \overline{M}$ $\overline{16}\ \overline{11}\ \overline{12}\ \overline{20}\ \overline{15}$ $\overline{17}$ $\overline{3}\ \overline{20}\ \overline{19}\ \overline{7}\ \overline{20}$ $\overline{12}\ \overline{11}$ $\overline{12}\ \overline{6}\ \overline{20}\ \overline{20}$

$\overline{14}$. $\overline{19}\ \overline{16}\ \overline{16}\ \overline{11}$

ON THE TABLE

Hint on page 47

Mrs. DeBuss loves to throw big parties. She places square tables together so that there is room for 1 person on each side of one table. Two tables can accommodate 6 people as shown. Three tables can handle 8 people, and so on. On Saturday, Mrs. DeBuss will be having a party for 32 people. How many tables will she need to put together?

Answer on page 49

Illustration: John Nez

22

HIDDEN NUMBERS

Illustration: Joe Seidita

SCRAMBLED PICTURE

Copy these mixed-up rectangles onto the next page to unscramble the picture.

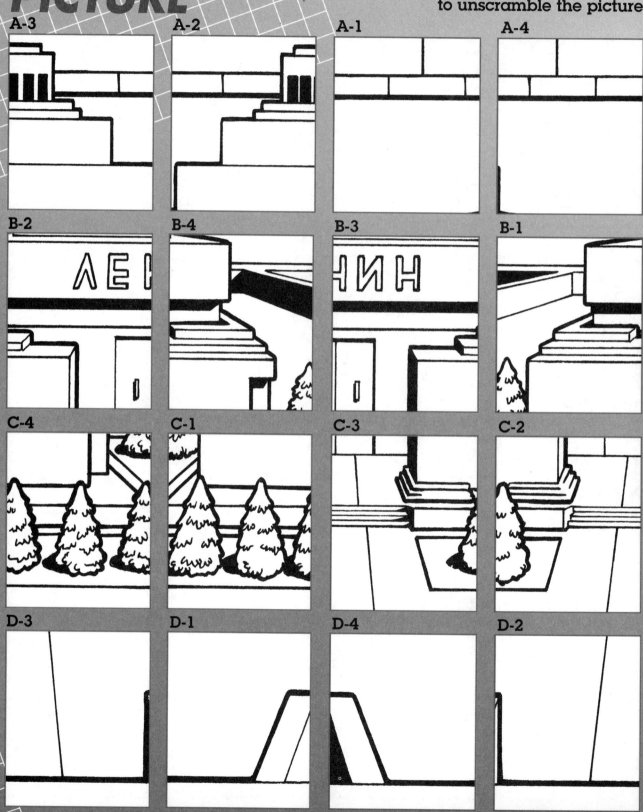

A-3 A-2 A-1 A-4

B-2 B-4 B-3 B-1

C-4 C-1 C-3 C-2

D-3 D-1 D-4 D-2

The letters and numbers tell you where each rectangle belongs. We've done the first one, A-3, to start you off.

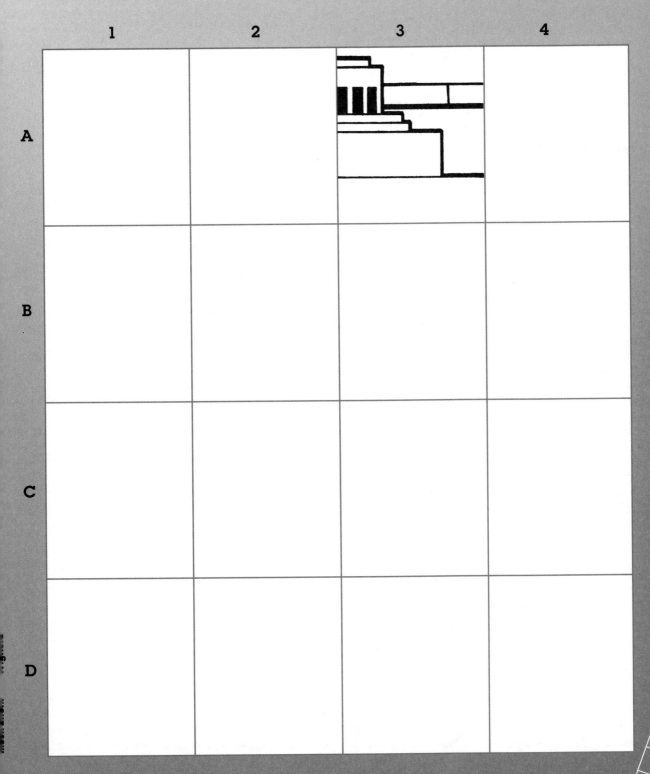

	1	2	3	4
A				
B				
C				
D				

Answer on page 49

LOAD IT UP

Leon drives down to the store every week. He always buys the same number of bags of horse feed and pig feed. But he buys twice as many bags of chicken feed. How many bags of each type of feed does he buy if he always fills his trailer to its capacity?

HORSE FEED
100 POUNDS

PIG FEED
50 POUNDS

CHICKEN FEED
25 POUNDS

Answer on page 50

400 POUNDS
MAXIMUM LOAD

26

POST LINES

Hint on page 47

Rasheed is trying to connect these nine posts by using only four straight lines. Can you show him how to do it?

Illustration: Doug Cushman

CROSSWORD RIDDLE

Fill in these boxes with the letters of the words that answer each clue or description. When you've completed the grid, rearrange the letters in the yellow boxes to discover the answer to our riddle.

ACROSS

1. The next hour after 12
2. Number of feet on a quadruped
5. Abbreviation for *Maine*
6. 6 in roman numerals
7. Another name for the twos in a deck of cards
10. A group of three people
12. Girl's name
15. Devices that weigh things such as fruit
18. 99 in roman numerals
20. 1st, 2nd, 3___, 4th
21. $\frac{3}{4}$ of a dozen
22. The final answer in an addition problem

DOWN

1. Opposite of a number that is even
2. 24 inches equals two of these.
3. Abbreviation for *ultraviolet*
4. Island in the Caribbean Sea: Puerto ____
5. 1100 in roman numerals
8. Inventor of the cotton gin: ____ Whitney
9. Abbreviation for *senior*
11. What water becomes at 32° Fahrenheit or lower
12. One of an identical pair
13. The letters at the top and bottom of a compass
14. Measure of land equal to 4840 square yards
16. Abbreviation for *anno Domini* when referring to a year
17. Short for *Samuel* or *Samantha*
19. 101 in roman numerals

Answer on page 50

The more you use this, the more you get:

_ _ _ _ _ _ _ _ _ _ _ _ .

RIGHT ROUTE

Rhonda likes to ride her bicycle so much that she doesn't always take the most direct route.

7TH AVENUE

4TH STREET

RHONDA'S ROUTE
1 block north
2 blocks west
1 block south
1 block west
2 blocks south
2 blocks east
1 block north
3 blocks east
2 blocks north
1 block west
Enter nearest building

Illustration: Rick Geary

Can you follow her path and figure out which store she visited?

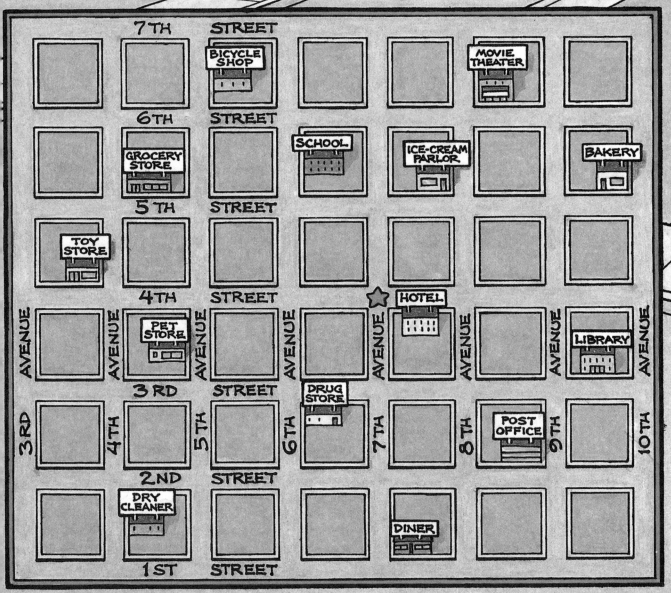

Answer on page 50

Hint on page 47

ADD A SIGN

Hint on page 47

TAILOR-MADE

Bob N. Sew, the town tailor, was dividing a piece of cloth into 1-yard lengths. He found that he cut at the speed of 1 yard per second. The piece of cloth he started with was 60 yards long. How long did it take him to finish cutting?

Illustration: Ron LeHew

Answer on page 50

Hint on page 47

33

SHAPE SPLITS

Pizzas come in all sorts of shapes in this place. Each pizza here has already been cut into pieces, and some pieces have been eaten. Can you give the fractional amount of the pieces that are already gone?

Answer on page 50

A

B

C

D

For example, there are 10 pieces in this shape on the right. That number becomes the denominator, or bottom number, in our fraction. There are 3 pieces shaded. That 3 becomes the top number, or numerator, in our fraction. So the proper fraction for this shape is $\frac{3}{10}$, or three-tenths. How many other fractions can you find?

E

F

G

H

MATHMAGIC

This trick is as easy as 1, 2, and especially 3!

Have a friend think of any number, but make sure he keeps it secret.

Ask him to multiply it by 3. Then tell him to add 1 to this new total.

Now have him multiply the new number by 3.

Ask him to add his original number to this new total.

He may now tell you his final number. And now you will be ready to tell him his original number.

How can you do it? Turn to page 50 to find out.

Illustration: Marc Nadel

PRECISE ICE

A true champion will be able to skate over this figure without crossing over or doubling back along any lines.

Illustration: Barbara Gray

Answer on page 50

STRIKE ONE

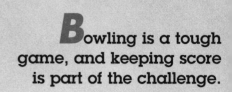

Bowling is a tough game, and keeping score is part of the challenge.

The numbers in the small boxes are the numbers of pins knocked down in each frame. These new pins should be added to the total from the frame before. Then this new number is placed in the bigger section of the box in each frame.

For example, here are the first three frames of Rocky's game:

	Frame 1	Frame 2	Frame 3
	8	6	5
Rocky	8	14	19

See how the 6 in the second frame was added to the 8 to make 14? And then the 5 was added to raise the score to 19.

A / is a spare, which means all the pins were knocked down in two tries. The score in that box includes all 10 pins for that frame plus the number of pins knocked down on the very first ball of the next frame.

For example:

	Frame 3	Frame 4	Frame 5
	5	/	4/0
Rocky	19	33	37

Rocky's score went up to 37 in this way: 19 + 10 (for all the pins that were knocked down in the 4th frame) + 4 (for the number of pins knocked down by the first ball in the 5th frame). That 4 was added in again in the 5th frame for a new score of 37.

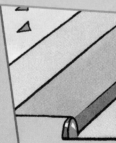

An X is a strike, which means all the pins were knocked down on the first try.

For example:

	Frame 4	Frame 5	Frame 6	Frame 7
	/	4/0	X	2/5
Rocky	33	37	54	61

Rocky's score went up to 61 in this way: 37 + 10 (for all the pins that were knocked down in the 6th frame) + 7 (for the total amount knocked down by both balls in the 7th frame). That 7 was added in again in the 7th frame for a new score of 61.

Can you use the scoreboard
and the examples to figure
out who won this game?

	Frame 1	Frame 2	Frame 3	Frame 4	Frame 5	Frame 6	Frame 7	Frame 8	Frame 9	Frame 10	Final Score
Ali	5	9	X	4/5	6	8	8	/	5/0	9	
Layne	6	9	8	7	/	6/3	X	4/2	7	5	

KINGPINS

Illustration: Ron Zalme

Answer on page 51

MATHMANIA

LIBRARY LAUGHS

Dewey has some funny books in his library. To check one out, solve each problem. Then go to the shelves to find the volume with the number that matches each answer. Put the matching letter in the blank beside each answer. Read down the letters you've filled in to find the title and author of the book Dewey just finished reading.

Illustration: Scott Peck

$5 + 4 =$ _____ _____

$3 \times 6 =$ _____ _____

$30 \div 2 =$ _____ _____

$7 - 6 =$ _____ _____

$7 + 6 =$ _____ _____

$8 - 6 =$ _____ _____

$5 \times 5 =$ _____ _____

$19 - 4 =$ _____ _____

$24 \div 2 =$ _____ _____

$16 - 7 =$ _____ _____

$11 \times 2 =$ _____ _____

$4 + 1 =$ _____ _____

$9 \times 2 =$ _____ _____

$12 \div 3 =$ _____ _____

$21 - 5 =$ _____ _____

$2 \times 6 =$ _____ _____

$1 \times 1 =$ _____ _____

$27 \div 3 =$ _____ _____

$15 + 4 =$ _____ _____

$22 - 3 =$ _____ _____

Hint on page 47

Answer on page 51

COLOR BY NUMBERS

Use the key to color the spaces and you'll find who's monkeying around.

Illustration: Joe Wigfield

Answer on page 51

KEY

1 dot—Gray   4 dots—Light Green
2 dots—Black   5 dots—Dark Green
3 dots—Yellow   6 dots—Blue

WEIGHT AND SEE

These animals want to send some items to friends in other places. They've all weighed in, but now

48 Pounds

7.2 Pounds

8.2 Pounds

73 Pounds

9 Pounds

1 Pound

15 Pounds

3.6 Pounds

.8 Pound

7 Pounds

1.2 Pound.

they need to pay the shipping charges. Use the chart to help them find the right dollar amounts.

ANIMAL AIR SHIPPING FEES

WEIGHT	CHARGE
0-1 pound	$3.30
1.1-3 pounds	$3.75
3.1-6 pounds	$5.50
6.1-10 pounds	$7.50
10.1-20 pounds	$14.35
20.1-40 pounds	$18.35
40.1-100 pounds	$28.35

Illustration: David Helton

Hint on page 47

5 Pounds

4.5 Pounds

8.1 Pounds

.2 Pound

1.7 Pounds

.6 Pound

9.7 Pounds

MAMA

68 Pounds

1.8 Pounds

Answer on page 51

COUNT ON IT

The sign below might not make much sense to you now, but it will help you answer this customer's question. Just fill in the blanks with the appropriate letter from the sign.

CUT ROOM SALE GOAL NOW!!

Got any cats going cheap?

16th letter: ____
5th letter: ____
9th letter: ____
15th letter: ____
10th letter: ____
13th letter: ____
2nd letter: ____
4th letter: ____
1st letter: ____
14th letter: ____
3rd letter: ____
8th letter: ____
12th letter: ____
17th letter: ____
7th letter: ____
11th letter: ____
6th letter: ____
18th letter: ____

Illustration: Arieh Zeldich

Hint on page 47

Answer on page 51

CUTUPS

Lumber Jackie is trying to divide this board into four different sections that have the same shape and value. No piece can have the same two digits in it.

Illustration: Rocky Fuller

1	1	2	5
3	4	4	6
8	2	8	2
1	2	1	4
3	7	5	3

Hint on page 47

Answer on page 51

HINTS AND BRIGHT IDEAS

*T*hese hints may help with some of the trickier puzzles.

COMMON BONDS (page 3)
It has to do with size, not value. Writing out the word for each number may help.

COUNTING SHEEP (pages 4-5)
Is there a quick way to find the number of sheep without counting each one individually?

IN GOOD SHAPE (page 10)
The missing numbers range from 3 to 16, though not all are included.

CRUNCH AND MUNCH (page 14)
8 ounces is the same as $\frac{1}{2}$ pound. There are 16 ounces in 1 pound.

MONEY-MAKER (pages 16-17)
To find the value, add the coins together. For example, 1 quarter, 2 dimes, 3 nickels, and 4 pennies is $.25 + $.20 + $.15 + $.04, or $.64. It may help to get a pile of coins and count each combination.

LET'S RE-COOP (page 18)
When put together correctly, the three will form four.

ALL ALIKE (page 19)
One of the operations is multiplication. Try multiplying the first number times the second.

DIGIT DOES IT (pages 20-21)
The word *Inspector* appears in the note's greeting. Use the code numbers from this word to help figure out the rest of the message.

ON THE TABLE (page 22)

Subtract the 2 people who will sit at either end. Now divide the remaining number of guests by the number of people who can sit on either side of each square table when the tables are together.

POST LINES (page 27)

Think beyond the limits of the nine posts.

CROSSWORD RIDDLE (pages 28-29)

CI is the roman numeral for 101. IC is the roman numeral for 99. M is the roman numeral for 1000. *Tina* is the girl's name. *UV* is short for "ultraviolet."

RIGHT ROUTE (pages 30-31)

If you're not sure where to begin, look at the picture for a clue.

ADD A SIGN (page 32)

Remember, you are adding only one symbol somewhere to the left of the = sign. For the first one, try putting a + sign between 572 and 43.

TAILOR-MADE (page 33)

Don't get sidetracked by the yards. All you are doing is figuring out how much time it took to cut the cloth into 60 equal pieces. This is tricky, though, because of the final cut.

LIBRARY LAUGHS (page 40)

Remember to consult the books to find the letter that matches each number.

WEIGHT AND SEE (pages 42-43)

Add numbers with decimal points (.) as if they were regular numbers, and then just put a decimal point before the last number in your total. For example, add 3.2, 9.5, and 7.1 like this: 32 + 95 + 71 = 198. Put the decimal point before the last number to get 19.8. Items with tags that have matching dots are being shipped together.

COUNT ON IT (page 44)

To save time, you might want to number the letters on the sign.

CUTUPS (page 45)

Each piece will have five numbers that add up to 18. Each shape will include a 1 and a 2 inside.

ANSWERS

COVER
9 + 0, 8 + 1, 7 + 2, 6 + 3, 5 + 4

COMMON BONDS (page 3)
3, 7, 8, 40, 50, and 60 are the only numbers that have just five letters.
1, 2, 6, and 10 are the only numbers that have just three letters.

COUNTING SHEEP (pages 4-5)
There are 39 sheep. A quick way to find the number of sheep is to count the groups and then multiply by 3.

SIMONE SAYS (page 6)

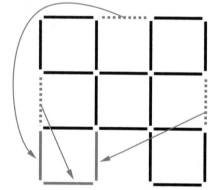

TAKE OFF (page 7)
A. 13 should be 14. Count by 3s.
B. 56 should be 60. Count by 5s.
C. 25 should be 23. Count down by 4s.
D. 5 should be 6. Count by $1\frac{1}{2}$s.

EYE TEST (pages 8-9)
A. Yes
B. Yes
C. Both curves are equal in size.
D. 1

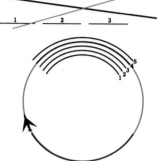

E. 4

IN GOOD SHAPE (page 10)
A. 9 + 3 = 12, 9 − 3 = 6
B. 10 + 7 = 17, 10 − 7 = 3
C. 8 + 6 = 14, 8 − 6 = 2
D. 16 + 4 = 20, 16 − 4 = 12
E. 8 + 5 = 13, 8 − 5 = 3
F. 11 + 7 = 18, 11 − 7 = 4

DOTS A LOT (page 11)

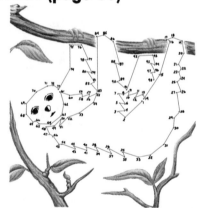

PARKING SPACES (pages 12-13)

CRUNCH AND MUNCH (page 14)

Purple Peanut Puffs
  2 pounds = 4 breakfasts
Flaky Flakes
  $3\frac{1}{2}$ pounds = 7 breakfasts
Chocolate Sugar Screamers
  $2\frac{1}{2}$ pounds = 5 breakfasts
Mini Micro Marshmallows
  48 ounces = 6 breakfasts
Seaweed and Succotash Smacks
  64 ounces = 8 breakfasts

FAMOUS NAME (page 15)

THOMAS EDISON

MONEY-MAKER (pages 16-17)

1	2	3	4	5	6	7	8	9	10
11	12	13	14	15	16	17	18	19	20
21	22	23	24	25	26	27	28	29	30
31	32	33	34	35	36	37	38	39	40
41	42	43	44	45	46	47	48	49	50
51	52	53	54	55	56	57	58	59	60
61	62	63	64	65	66	67	68	69	70
71	72	73	74	75	76	77	78	79	80
81	82	83	84	85	86	87	88	89	90
91	92	93	94	95	96	97	98	99	100

LET'S RE-COOP (page 18)

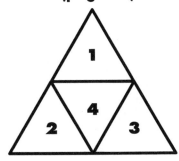

ALL ALIKE (page 19)

$3 \times 6 - 8 = 10$ $7 \times 2 - 4 = 10$
$5 \times 4 - 10 = 10$ $6 \times 5 - 20 = 10$
$2 \times 9 - 8 = 10$ $3 \times 5 - 5 = 10$

DIGIT DOES IT (pages 20-21)

Dear Inspector Digit,
You've horned in, so I must flee.
To be instrumental in catching me,
Look sharp and try to see
The 25 notes I leave to thee.
P. Anno

a-19	f-4	l-3	r-18	y-9
b-2	g-10	m-5	s-15	
c-13	h-6	n-16	t-12	
d-1	i-17	o-11	u-8	
e-20	k-21	p-14	v-7	

ON THE TABLE (page 22)

15 tables

HIDDEN NUMBERS (page 23)

SCRAMBLED PICTURE (pages 24-25)

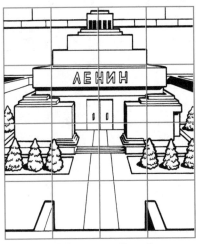

Lenin's tomb in Moscow, Russia

LOAD IT UP (page 26)
2 bags of horse feed, 2 bags of pig feed, and 4 bags of chicken feed

POST LINES (page 27)

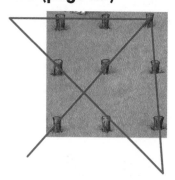

CROSSWORD RIDDLE (pages 28-29)

The more you use this, the more you get: ADDITION.

RIGHT ROUTE (pages 30-31)

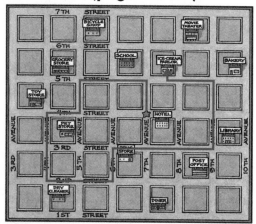

Rhonda visited the ice-cream parlor.

ADD A SIGN (page 32)
A. 572 + 43 = 615
B. 284 × 2 = 568
C. 41 + 389 = 430
D. 861 − 98 = 763
E. 92 × 10 = 920
F. 862 ÷ 2 = 431
G. 97 + 86 = 183
H. 465 − 32 = 433
I. 201 × 4 = 804

TAILOR-MADE (page 33)
It took 59 seconds. The final cut made 2 separate pieces.

SHAPE SPLITS (pages 34-35)
A. $\frac{2}{3}$

B. $\frac{1}{4}$

C. $\frac{1}{2}$

D. $\frac{5}{6}$

E. $\frac{2}{5}$

F. $\frac{5}{8}$

G. $\frac{4}{7}$

H. $\frac{3}{4}$

MATHMAGIC (page 36)
Your friend's final number will always end in 3. Just ignore that last 3, and the other number or numbers will make up your friend's original. For example, let's say his original number was 25; 25 × 3 = 75; 75 + 1 = 76; 76 × 3 = 228; 228 + 25 = 253. Take away the 3, and you're left with 25.

PRECISE ICE (page 37)

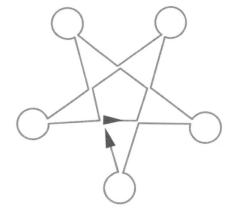